Who Is
Malala Yousafzai?

Who Is Malala Yousafzai?

By Dinah Brown
Illustrated by Andrew Thomson

SCHOLASTIC INC.

ISBN 978-0-545-90227-4

12 11 10 9 8 7 6 5 4 3 2 1   15 16 17 18 19 20/0

Printed in the U.S.A.   40

First Scholastic printing, September 2015

Contents

Who Is
Malala Yousafzai?

When Malala Yousafzai (mah-LAH-lah yoo-sahf-ZIGH) was a little girl in Mingora, Pakistan, she decided to be a doctor when she grew up. She knew she would have to go to school for many years and study very hard. But Malala didn't mind at all. She loved everything about school. She loved reading. She loved history and geography and science. She loved studying religion. She enjoyed writing and reading stories aloud to her classmates.

When her teacher talked about something new,
she couldn't wait to learn more. Tests were
difficult, but they were fun, too, especially when
she had studied hard and knew the answers.

Then, when Malala was ten years old, her life
changed. War came to Mingora, the city where
she lived. A group of violent fighters called the
Taliban had taken over her beloved Swat Valley.
They were saying that girls would soon be stopped
from going to school. Not boys. Just girls.

The Taliban started destroying girls' schools. The Pakistan Army arrived to stop them. Mingora became a war zone. It was very dangerous. People were afraid to go out.

Malala wondered how she could ever become a doctor if she wasn't allowed to learn. She wished there was something she could do to help keep her school open. Many were closed, and few students dared to go to the ones that were open. But Malala went to school every day.

Malala spoke out. She told local newspapers that she was afraid the Taliban would close her school. She talked about how frightening her life had become. She said that more than anything, she wanted to go to school.

Malala was becoming famous. People were talking about her. Some Taliban fighters learned her name and decided to take revenge. On October 9, 2012, two of them stopped her school bus. One walked around to the back and looked inside. Then he shot Malala.

Malala Yousafzai was lucky to survive. She was flown to a hospital where she recovered.

Did she stop speaking out?

No.

When she was better, she went on working for the right of all children to be educated. But she never stopped learning and studying and going to school.

On July 12, 2013, she addressed hundreds

of young people at the United Nations Youth Assembly in New York City. "So here I stand, one girl among many," she said. "I speak—not for myself, but for all girls and boys. I raise up my voice—not so that I can shout, but so that those without a voice can be heard."

Malala Yousafzai wanted one thing—an education. She spoke up, and people listened. Things began to change, little by little, until the whole world was listening.

Chapter 1
A Girl Is Born

On July 12, 1997, Malala Yousafzai was born in the city of Mingora, Pakistan. Outside her parents' bedroom, a new day was about to begin. Soon the city would come alive with horns honking and people calling and music playing. But now it was early. The morning sun was rising behind the mountains outside the city. A rooster crowed. A scooter's engine revved.

Like many families in their poor neighborhood, the Yousafzais couldn't afford a doctor or midwife. Instead, a neighbor woman arrived to deliver the baby. When Tor Pekai Yousafzai was handed her first child, she felt instant love. But there was also sadness in her heart. Tor Pekai knew what was in store for this little girl. Her friends and neighbors in Mingora would not celebrate her birth. If she had been a boy, they would have brought gifts and food and poems.

Tor Pekai had grown up in a remote mountain village. Most girls did not go to school. However, Tor Pekai wanted to learn. When she was six, she went to the village school, but being a girl in school was so unusual that she soon left.

In Mingora and many other areas of the Swat Valley, it was common for all children to attend school. The first girls' school was built in the 1920s. High schools and colleges followed. The rulers believed that all children, girls as well as boys, should be educated. Pakistan was proud of the graduates in the Swat area who went on to become teachers, doctors, and other professionals.

Malala's father had also grown up in a mountain village. He also believed in schooling for girls. When Ziauddin (zee-OW-dun) saw his new baby daughter, he did not feel disappointed. He felt proud. He would make sure that she would have the same chances in life as any boy.

Three years earlier, he had built a private
elementary school for boys and girls. He called it
the Khushal School. He was the teacher. Ziauddin
planned to build more schools, then more and
more. A high school for girls, another for boys,
until every child in Mingora had a place to learn.

Ziauddin had grown up in a religious Muslim family. His father was a teacher. He taught Ziauddin that children were sacred, and all children needed to learn. He explained that it was important to help others. Ziauddin listened.

ISLAM

ISLAM IS A PEACEFUL RELIGION PRACTICED
BY MORE THAN A BILLION PEOPLE AROUND
THE WORLD. MUSLIMS ARE FOLLOWERS OF THE
ISLAMIC FAITH. ISLAM TEACHES THERE IS ONE
GOD, KNOWN AS ALLAH IN THE ARABIC LAN-
GUAGE. THE WORDS OF ALLAH ARE REVEALED
IN THE SACRED BOOK OF ISLAM, CALLED THE
QURAN. MUSLIM HOUSES OF WORSHIP ARE CALLED
MOSQUES.

Ziauddin had been small for his age. His skin was darker than the other children. He'd stuttered when he tried to speak out in class. Sometimes children had bullied or ignored him. Sometimes he had felt like an outsider.

Many people tried to get him to join dangerous groups. They wanted him to think in a certain way. The more he read, the more he learned how to make up his own mind. When he grew up, he realized that school had saved him.

At Malala's birth, Ziauddin looked down at his new daughter and wondered what her name should be. This child must be named for a strong, free woman. Ziauddin studied his family tree. It went back for three hundred years. Yet he could not find one girl's name listed. But in his Pashtun culture, there were so many heroines, so many names to choose from. In the end he decided to name this baby after a brave young girl—Malalai of Maiwand—who loved her country greatly.

THE PASHTUN PEOPLE

THE PASHTUN PEOPLE LIVE IN THE COUNTRY OF AFGHANISTAN AND IN THE NORTHWEST CORNER OF PAKISTAN. MANY LIVE IN THE MOUNTAINS AND ARE USED TO A RUGGED LIFE.

THROUGHOUT HISTORY, THE PASHTUN PEOPLE HAVE STRUGGLED TO FIGHT OFF MANY ENEMIES. THE PASHTUN ARE PROUD PEOPLE. THEY HAVE NOT WANTED TO LOSE THEIR TRADITIONS. THEY BELIEVE IN RESPECT AND GENEROSITY TOWARD OTHERS. THEY VALUE LOYALTY TO FAMILY, FRIENDS, AND NEIGHBORS. ALMOST ALL PASHTUN PEOPLE FOLLOW THE ISLAMIC RELIGION.

He raised his pen and wrote his new daughter's name: *Malala*.

MALALAI OF MAIWAND

THERE WAS ONCE A GIRL NAMED MALALAI. SHE
LIVED IN A TINY TOWN IN AFGHANISTAN, NOT FAR
FROM PAKISTAN. MALALAI WAS THE DAUGHTER OF
A SHEPHERD. IN 1880, THE BRITISH WERE TRYING
TO TAKE OVER AFGHANISTAN. MANY LOCAL BOYS
AND MEN JOINED THE BATTLE TO STOP THEM.
MALALAI'S FATHER AND THE MAN SHE LOVED
FOUGHT, TOO. THE BATTLE OF MAIWAND TOOK
PLACE NEAR MALALAI'S HOME. MALALAI HELPED
CARE FOR WOUNDED AFGHAN SOLDIERS. MALALAI
WAS AFRAID FOR THE MEN. SHE DID NOT WANT
THEM TO GIVE UP. SO SHE TOOK OFF HER VEIL
AND WAVED IT. THEN SHE BEGAN TO SING.

WITH A DROP OF MY SWEETHEART'S BLOOD
SHED IN DEFENSE OF THE MOTHERLAND,
WILL I PUT A BEAUTY SPOT ON MY FOREHEAD,
SUCH AS WOULD PUT TO SHAME
THE ROSE IN THE GARDEN.

THE AFGHAN SOLDIERS HEARD HER SONG.
THEY FOUGHT HARDER AND WON THE BATTLE.
BUT DURING IT, MALALAI WAS SHOT AND KILLED.
MALALAI OF MAIWAND IS A HERO. SHE IS THE
GIRL WHO HELPED TURN THE TIDE AND STOP
THE BRITISH.

Chapter 2
Born with Wings

When Malala was two, her brother Khushal was born. The neighbors brought gifts and food and laughter. This baby boy's future was full of possibilities, they said as they celebrated. He might even go to a university. Maybe he would become a doctor, or a teacher like his father.

Ziauddin was aware that Malala was listening. He was a polite man. He did not wish to offend his guests by pointing out that the schools he was building in Mingora were for boys *and* girls. Maybe Khushal and Malala would *both* go to a university and become doctors.

Malala loved her father's schoolroom. Sometimes, when she was little, she stood at the front of the empty classroom and pretended she was a teacher.

As Malala grew older, she enjoyed helping her mother prepare meals. When the family moved from their cramped rooms by the school, she couldn't wait to help her mother in their new garden.

There was more space now. On most evenings, neighbors gathered on the porch and ate the food that Malala had helped prepare.

Sometimes she sat with the women. They talked about their day and watched the sun set over the mountains that rose up beyond the lakes and pastures in the beautiful Swat Valley.

But most of the time, she joined the men. She
loved listening to them swap stories and talk about
politics. Often, her father recited poetry or spoke
of heroes like her namesake, Malalai. Sometimes
he recited poems by his favorite poet, Rumi.

Later, Malala would say that her father allowed
her to grow. "He didn't give me something extra,"

she said, "but he never clipped my wings. He let me fly. He let me achieve my goals."

THE POEMS OF RUMI

MALALA GREW UP LISTENING TO THE POEMS OF THE GREAT POET RUMI. RUMI WAS BORN ON SEPTEMBER 30, 1207, IN WHAT IS NOW THE COUNTRY OF AFGHANISTAN. HE SPOKE AND WROTE ABOUT WHAT HE THOUGHT WAS MOST IMPORTANT IN LIFE. HERE ARE SOME OF HIS SAYINGS.

IGNORE THOSE THAT MAKE YOU FEARFUL
AND SAD.

I WANT TO SING LIKE THE BIRDS SING,
NOT WORRYING ABOUT WHO HEARS OR
WHAT THEY THINK.

DON'T BE SATISFIED WITH STORIES,
HOW THINGS HAVE GONE WITH OTHERS.
UNFOLD YOUR OWN MYTH.

BE A LAMP, OR A LIFEBOAT, OR A LADDER.
HELP SOMEONE'S SOUL HEAL. WALK OUT OF
YOUR HOUSE LIKE A SHEPHERD.

INSIDE YOU THERE'S AN ARTIST YOU DON'T
KNOW ABOUT.

Chapter 3
At Home in Mingora

By the time Malala's second brother, Atal, was born, more than eight hundred children were studying in Ziauddin's schools. One elementary school for boys and girls. One high school for boys.

One high school for girls. Malala was seven and
Khushal was almost five when the new baby
came.

Like most families in Pakistan, the whole
family ate their meals together. Breakfast was
served very early. Men and boys went to a nearby
mosque, a place of worship, to pray. Women and
girls said prayers at home.

In her father's school, Malala took many
courses. She studied three languages—Pashto,
English, and Urdu, the official language of
Pakistan. She learned math, science, history, and
Islamic studies.

Her mother, Tor Pekai, was anxious to learn, too. She couldn't read or write, but she enjoyed listening to her daughter talk about what she had learned at school that day.

Like most of the children in her classes, Malala spoke Pashto at home. At school, the teachers taught in English and Urdu. Soon Malala was able to speak and understand all three languages.

Some families paid a few dollars a month for their children to attend Ziauddin's low-cost private schools. Other children could not afford to pay anything, but her father welcomed them anyway.

Ziauddin and his family had a little more money now. They bought CDs and books. Malala loved to read. After finishing the Twilight series, she thought it would be fun to be a vampire!

The Yousafzais also bought a TV. Sometimes they watched shows from Islamabad, the capital of Pakistan. And once in a while there were shows from faraway countries, like England, Australia, and America. *Ugly Betty*, a show about a girl who worked at a magazine, was one of Malala's favorites.

Malala began to see that people spoke and dressed and acted differently in different places.

Her parents explained that people may look different, but what matters is who they are inside.

Malala loved going to the market with her mother. There were so many different stalls to visit. She bought small toys and sweets and shiny bracelets. She examined the colorful scarves and the newest DVDs. She watched the cobbler making shoes and helped her mother pick out fruits and vegetables.

As she grew older, she began to spend more
time with the women and less time with the men.
But often, she served the men tea and stayed to
listen. When she was eight and nine, there seemed
to be more talk about politics than poetry, and the
more she heard, the more interested she became.

Someone mentioned the war in the neighboring country of Afghanistan. A strict and violent group in power—the Taliban—made women obey severe laws. Girls and women could not leave the house unless they were with a man. And the man had to be a relative. Women could not work outside the home. Girls could not go to school. Many women who disobeyed the Taliban's laws had been badly beaten or put to death.

Someone else mentioned a man on a local radio station. He was talking about stopping all girls in Mingora from going to school.

Malala couldn't believe it. How could anyone say that girls shouldn't go to school? Unlike her brother Khushal, she enjoyed homework and writing papers and studying for tests. She had won many prizes for earning the highest grades or being the best in her class. She loved all the schoolbooks her father had found for his students to read. She loved speaking in front of the class and seeing her friends every day. Her friend Moniba, most of all. Moniba was smart, too. Often, she and Malala would get into silly fights. But that didn't mean they weren't best friends.

Malala couldn't imagine what her life would be like if she couldn't go to school. She was afraid.

Chapter 4
Dangerous Times

When Malala was little, there were many tourists in the Swat Valley. Some came for the summer music and dance festivals. Others sat by the Swat River or climbed in the mountains. Often, they did not dress the same as the people in Swat. Malala knew that women and girls in different parts of the world followed different customs.

Malala also knew that the Swat region was not as modern as some places in Pakistan. There were women in the big city of Islamabad who dressed like the women in Europe and the United States that she had seen on TV. Most women and girls in Mingora did not dress that way. They wrapped their bodies in scarves or cloaks when they went out.

They wore head scarves. In her mother's mountain village, women often dressed in an even more traditional way. They chose to wear a cloth garment called a burqa (BUR-ka) whenever they left the house. The burqa covered their whole body and face, with a cutout so they could see.

In 2007, Malala was ten years old. By this time, members of the Taliban were taking over the Swat Valley. They said that all women had to wear burqas. The Taliban wanted to take away freedom from all women. On a radio station, a Taliban man was shouting frightening things.

He announced that, besides wearing burqas, girls and women in Mingora should stay at home. They could no longer go to the market alone. They could only go out with a male relative. Women who did not follow these rules would be punished.

Was that all?

No!

Women would not be able to vote. They could not hold jobs. There would no longer be female doctors, and women weren't allowed to go to male doctors. They could not go to hospitals. That meant there was no way for sick women to be treated. Music and dancing were banned. All televisions and CDs and computers would be burned. Only religious books could be read. Girls' schools would be destroyed if they were not closed.

Teachers and principals who continued to teach girls would be punished.

The man was saying that good Muslims would never allow girls to go to school. Malala knew that wasn't true. Her family and friends and neighbors were all good Muslims. They were deeply religious. They prayed every day. They also believed that every child should be educated. At her religious school, Malala had learned that Muslims believed in peace and kindness to others.

One evening a man came to Malala's house and told Ziauddin to close his girls' high school. Malala's father refused. Malala was afraid. What if something happened to her father?

Other schools were destroyed. The Taliban were breaking into homes. They were searching for "illegal" books. They were destroying TVs and video games. They closed the movie theaters and places where people had gone to listen to music and dance.

Female doctors and teachers were leaving the area to find work in safer places. Women were no longer at the market, and men were afraid, so many of the shops were closing. Men were no longer allowed to shave. Barbershops were closing, too.

Men with guns—Taliban members—were everywhere. People were frightened to go outside. Ziauddin kept his schools open, but many students were afraid of the Taliban and stayed home.

At the end of 2007, the Pakistan Army arrived to stop the Taliban. Mingora and most of the Swat Valley became a war zone. There was bombing at night and during the day. Most people stayed in their homes. But some children continued to go to school. Malala was one of them.

Fighting between the Pakistani soldiers and the Taliban went on through much of 2008. After many months, it seemed like the army was winning. Everybody hoped that the Taliban was gone for good. Life would soon get back to normal.

The Pakistan Army moved out of the Swat Valley. But the Taliban had not gone away. The radio threats had started again. People who did not follow orders were severely punished. Shops were burned. By the end of 2008, more than 150 girls' schools in Mingora were destroyed.

Malala realized her school was in danger. She also knew that she was lucky. If her school closed, her father would still continue to teach her. He would find math and science books and literature for her to read. But most girls in Mingora were not as lucky as she was. What would happen to them?

Chapter 5
A Secret Diary

In December, Malala's worst fear came true. An order came from the Taliban: Girls' schools in Mingora would not reopen after the winter break. The Taliban said boys could go back to school, but girls would not be returning. Malala and her friends were devastated. Could this be true? What would life be like if they couldn't go to school?

One day a BBC reporter in Pakistan asked Ziauddin for help. The BBC Urdu website was looking for a teacher to write about the school closings in Mingora. Ziauddin talked to some teachers, but they refused. They were afraid of the Taliban. Writing about what was happening in their city was much too dangerous.

Malala had spoken out before, and she had enjoyed it. In September 2008, she had given a speech at a local club for reporters. The title of her speech was "How Dare the Taliban Take Away My Basic Right to Education?" Newspapers all over Pakistan printed her words. She was glad to tell people how strongly she felt. She had said what she believed, and nothing bad had happened.

Ziauddin thought his daughter might be the perfect person to write the blog for the BBC. He asked Malala. She was only eleven. She didn't know much about writing journals, but she was ready to try it.

THE BBC

LIVE

LIVE PAKISTAN
BREAKING NEWS
Toliban troops destroy Swat Valley Schools
BBC NEWS   12:40 PAKISTAN

THE BRITISH BROADCASTING CORPORATION,
KNOWN AS THE BBC, IS BASED IN LONDON,
ENGLAND. IT BROADCASTS TV SHOWS, RADIO
PROGRAMS, AND WEBCASTS ALL OVER THE WORLD,
INCLUDING BBC AMERICA. JOURNALISTS FROM
THE BBC REPORT THE NEWS FROM ALL COUNTRIES
IN MANY DIFFERENT LANGUAGES. MALALA'S BLOG,
DIARY OF A PAKISTANI SCHOOLGIRL, WAS
ORIGINALLY PUBLISHED ON THE BBC URDU
WEBSITE.

Malala's parents talked it over with the man from the BBC. Everyone knew that Malala would do a good job. But there was much to consider.

Malala was worried that something bad might happen to her father if she wrote the blog. The man from the BBC was worried about Ziauddin, too. He was also worried about Malala.

Ziauddin wasn't worried about Malala. *No one would hurt a child*, he thought. That seemed impossible. Out of the question.

The man at the BBC talked to Malala and her parents many times. Finally, it was decided. Malala would write the blog, under one condition. She would use a fake name.

Malala's blog would be called *Diary of a Pakistani Schoolgirl*. She would use the name Gul Makai. This was the name of a strong girl in a famous Pashtun folktale. Malala would write notes and read them to the reporter every day on the phone. She would tell him how she and her friends were feeling and what was going on at home and in school. The reporter would put her words onto the website.

The BBC website started to publish *Diary of a Pakistani Schoolgirl* on January 3, 2009, in Urdu and in English. Other blog posts followed. Malala's words were about getting ready for school and studying for her tests. All the girls worried that school might not reopen after winter break.

There was bombing in the night, and the girls were afraid. They were afraid that their school would be destroyed, like so many other schools in Mingora. However, the Pakistan Army was fighting the Taliban. Maybe they would win and school wouldn't close after all.

At the same time, the *New York Times*
newspaper was making a film about the Taliban
who were taking over the Swat district and closing
girls' schools in Mingora. The film featured Malala
and her father. The cameras roamed Mingora
for six months, filming the fighting between
the Pakistan Army and the Taliban fighters.

Gunfire was heard everywhere. People were
desperate to get out of the city. Terrified men,
women, and children climbed onto the roofs of
overcrowded buses and trucks that were leaving.

Malala and Ziauddin talked about the bombs
that exploded outside their home night after
night, making it impossible to sleep. Malala said
her father could no longer walk her to school. It
was too dangerous for him to be seen outside. She
liked her blue school uniform, she said, but now
she couldn't wear it. The few students who still
attended dressed in plain clothes so the Taliban
wouldn't know where they were going.

Her school would soon close, she said, covering her face, trying not to cry. She wanted to be a doctor. Doctors must study for many years. How could she ever realize her dream if there was no school to go to?

In January 2009, the Taliban did the very thing that Malala had been dreading. All girls' schools would close for good on January 15. Boys' schools would stay open, but girls would have to remain at home.

On January 14, when school was over, Malala said good-bye to Moniba and all her other friends. No one knew what would happen next.

Malala spent the days reading, getting into fights with her brothers, and talking to the BBC reporter.

By February, *Diary of a Pakistani Schoolgirl* was being read all over Pakistan and in many other parts of the world. Malala continued writing it through March 12. The name Gul Makai was becoming well known in Swat. People wondered who it was. Malala didn't tell anyone.

Because Ziauddin had started schools for girls, many people wanted to interview him about what was happening in the Swat Valley. They wanted to talk to his daughter, too. Malala appeared on a Pakistani talk show. The host asked her questions about the war and school closings in Mingora.

Most people in Pakistan believed in education for girls. They were upset about what was happening in the Swat Valley. Many had read Malala's diary. The Taliban leaders had to listen. In February, it seemed as if the Taliban was having a change of heart. They announced that girls could go back to school. Malala and her friends couldn't wait to return to their studies. But even though some girls' schools were open again, the fighting in Mingora got worse. It was dangerous to walk in the city. Many students stayed home. Others left the city with their families.

By May, Ziauddin saw there was no choice. He closed his schools again. Malala and her family packed what they could and hurried out of Mingora.

They spent the next few months living in the houses of relatives in safer cities nearby. Malala missed her books, her friends, and especially her school. But she was glad to be away from Mingora and the sound of exploding bombs.

On July 24, the Yousafzai family finally returned home. Mingora was a bombed-out shell of what it had once been. The war was over, and the Taliban had moved into the hills. That was good. But the Taliban fighters knew who Malala was. She had spoken in public. She had been on TV. Many people had read her BBC diary or watched the *New York Times* film. People were talking about her.

In August, Malala's school finally reopened. Malala was too busy studying to worry about the Taliban. She had a new dream now. She wanted to become a politician. Politicians work to pass laws that they believe will benefit their country. Malala wanted to make sure that all children everywhere had the opportunity for an education.

Chapter 6
"Who Is Malala?"

By autumn of 2012, Mingora appeared to
have returned to normal. The Pakistan Army had
cleared the Taliban from the city. Once again,
the streets were alive with scooters and rickshaws.
Children were playing cricket outside. The
movie theater and barbershops had reopened.
Some of Malala's favorite shows were back on TV.

Many schools had been rebuilt, and the girls of Mingora had returned to their classrooms.

Malala had become famous. In 2011, the Dutch KidsRights foundation had nominated her for the International Children's Peace Prize. The prize is presented every year to a child "whose courageous or otherwise remarkable acts and thoughts have made a difference in countering problems which affect children around the world."

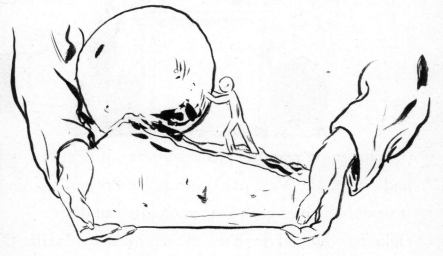

She did not win that year, but it was an honor simply to be recognized.

That same year, the prime minister of Pakistan
had started the National Youth Peace Prize.
It would be given each year to children under
eighteen who had done the most for peace. Malala
was awarded the prize. The name of the prize was
later changed to the National Malala Peace Prize.

Her family was proud of her, but they had become fearful. Malala rarely walked to or from school. Everyone knew that Taliban fighters had not gone far. They were out there somewhere, in the hills surrounding Mingora. No one was sure what they would do next.

On October 9, 2012, Malala was feeling
happy and proud as she climbed onto the small

school bus with her friends. She had studied hard for a test and thought she had done a good job. It was a warm fall day and the leaves were beginning to turn red and brown and yellow. Malala was fifteen years old.

Malala's small bus wasn't really a bus at all. It was more like a pickup truck with three rows of seats and a roof. The sides were covered, but the back of the bus was mostly open. The bus was crowded with high-school girls and three teachers. Malala was sitting next to her friend Moniba. Everyone had been singing and talking about tests. Suddenly the bus stopped, and a man with a gun leaned into the back of the bus.

"Who is Malala?" the man asked.

Some of the girls glanced at Malala. The man watched their eyes. He knew the girl they were looking at must be the girl he was searching for.

The man pointed the gun at Malala and pulled the trigger.

Malala remembered very little about what happened after that. She did not remember being shot in the head. She had no memory of the helicopter that flew her to the military hospital in Peshawar, Pakistan or her father arriving, or the surgery that saved her life. She was unaware of how sick she was after the operation, or the response to what had happened. Reporters gathered outside the hospital. Malala's picture appeared in newspapers all over the world. A local Taliban man had shot Malala, the articles said.

The news disgusted everyone, first in Pakistan, then everywhere. No one could believe that a young girl had been shot. A Muslim child being hurt like that was unheard of.

Malala was famous around the world now. Some of the stories made her sound almost too good to be true. But Malala was a regular girl. She liked Justin Bieber songs. Her favorite color was pink. She hated waking up early in the morning.

She spent lots of time creating different hairstyles for herself. She wished she wasn't so short. And she really enjoyed going to school—just like billions of other kids. Yet her love of learning was the reason she had been shot.

Malala was alive, yet remained very ill. Everyone at the hospital was worried about her. The operation was a success. Still, the doctors knew she would need the best care to recover completely. Malala was flown to a bigger hospital in Pakistan. She didn't remember that, either.

Soon Malala improved enough to be moved once again—this time to a hospital in Birmingham, England, that specialized in injuries like hers.

Chapter 7
All I Want Is an Education

On October 16, Malala woke up. A week before, she had been singing on a school bus in Mingora. Now she was in England, more than four thousand miles from home. Nothing seemed familiar.

Malala looked around and realized that she was in a hospital. The doctors and nurses were speaking English. She couldn't talk, because the doctors had put in a tube to help her breathe. Someone brought a board with the alphabet on it. Malala was able to spell out two words by pointing with her finger: *country* and *father*.

She was told that she was in England. Her father was coming soon with the rest of her family.

A few days later, her breathing tube was removed. The doctors didn't know if she would be able to speak. Everyone waited. Someone who spoke Urdu was called in. Malala started asking questions about where she was and what had happened. She remembered being on the school bus, but that was all. Was her mother coming? Her brothers? When would they arrive?

The doctors were delighted that she could speak. But it would take a long time for Malala to recover. She couldn't move her face properly. Her hearing had been damaged. She would need more operations.

When her family arrived, they lived in an apartment nearby. Later, when Malala was finally

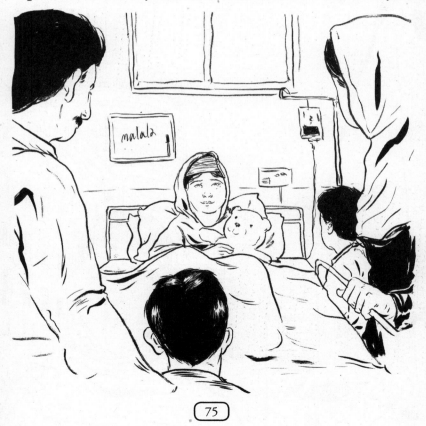

able to leave the hospital, they moved to a bigger
house in Birmingham, not far from the new
school that she would attend.

In order to get well, Malala needed months of
exercise and special workouts. She needed to take
walks, at first short, then longer and longer.

Sometimes, as she walked through the streets of Birmingham, she felt sad. She missed her home in Pakistan. Everything was so different. The clothes, the food, the shops, the weather. People were kind, but they were new friends who did not share her memories and stories. When she wasn't at school or doing her homework, she talked to Moniba and her other friends via Skype on her new computer.

Malala wondered if she would ever see Pakistan again.

It was difficult for the rest of the family, too. Leaving Pakistan had happened so fast. There hadn't been time to pack their favorite things. They missed all the visitors who had gathered at their home in Mingora. They missed watching the sun set over the mountains. They felt safe now, but they were also lonely. Everyone wondered when they would see their homeland again.

Chapter 8
Every Woman, Every Boy, Every Girl

The news of Malala's shooting spread quickly around the world. People everywhere were horrified. This young girl had wanted to go to school. She had written a diary. She had spoken out. She had asked the world to help her get an education. For this, she had nearly lost her life.

A month later, in November 2012, Ban Ki-moon, the secretary-general of the United Nations, declared that July 12, 2013,

BAN KI-MOON

Malala's sixteenth birthday, would be Malala Day at the United Nations.

Malala was invited to speak to the United Nations Youth Assembly in New York City. Every year, young people from all over the world meet with UN diplomats. They discuss what can be done to help children in their countries who are forced to work hard jobs at a very young age, and very young girls who are forced to marry. The diplomats learn about children like Malala, who are told they can no longer go to school.

By the summer of 2013, Malala was well enough to travel to the United States. She had spent nine months recovering from her injuries. The operation on her face had been a success. An operation to improve her hearing had also worked. Malala was ready to show the world that a terrorist with a gun had not stopped her. She would continue to speak out.

THE UNITED NATIONS

IN 1945, AT THE END OF WORLD WAR II, NATIONS ALL AROUND THE WORLD AGREED THAT THEY NEEDED A PLACE WHERE COUNTRIES COULD WORK TOGETHER TO HELP KEEP PEACE. THAT WAS THE PURPOSE OF THE UNITED NATIONS. IT WAS DECIDED THAT THE UNITED NATIONS' BUILDINGS WOULD BE LOCATED IN NEW YORK CITY. THE MOST FAMOUS ARE THE TALL GLASS SECRETARIAT BUILDING, AND THE DOMED GENERAL ASSEMBLY BUILDING. BY 2014, 193 COUNTRIES WERE MEMBERS OF THE UNITED NATIONS. DELEGATES GATHER IN THE GENERAL ASSEMBLY HALL. THEY CONSIDER MANY WORLD PROBLEMS—THE RIGHTS OF CHILDREN, POVERTY, COUNTRIES AT WAR. THEY LISTEN TO SPEAKERS AND VOTE. THE CHIEF OF THE UNITED NATIONS IS CALLED THE SECRETARY-GENERAL.

On July 12, 2013, Malala arrived at the United
Nations Headquarters with her family for the
daylong gathering. During the opening ceremony,
everyone sang "Happy Birthday" to her.

The room was crowded with diplomats and almost one thousand young people from around the world. As she walked to the podium, they rose to their feet and clapped.

Malala began to speak. She spoke in English. Her words were translated into many other languages through headphones. That way everyone in the room could understand.

"They thought that the bullets would silence us, but they failed," she said. "And out of that silence came thousands of voices. The terrorists thought they would change my aims and stop my ambitions. But nothing changed in my life except this: Weakness, fear, and hopelessness died. Strength, power, and courage was born."

Malala talked about what had happened to her nine months earlier. She did not hate the man who shot her. In fact, she would not shoot him if she had a gun. What she wanted to focus on was the need for peace. She mentioned Martin Luther King Jr., Mahatma Gandhi, and Mother Teresa, who had fought for their rights peacefully.

MARTIN LUTHER
KING JR.

Malala said, "Malala Day is not my day. Today is the day of every woman, every boy, and every girl who have raised their voice for their rights."

MAHATMA GANDHI (1869–1948)

MAHATMA GANDHI WAS A GREAT LEADER. HE SPENT HIS LIFE TRYING TO HELP THE PEOPLE OF INDIA. INDIA WAS RULED BY GREAT BRITAIN AT THE TIME. MANY PEOPLE WANTED TO CHANGE THAT. THEY BELIEVED INDIA SHOULD RULE ITSELF. SOME PEOPLE THOUGHT INDIA SHOULD GO TO WAR WITH GREAT BRITAIN. BUT GANDHI DIDN'T BELIEVE IN WAR. HE DIDN'T BELIEVE IN VIOLENCE. HE FELT THAT CHANGE SHOULD COME THROUGH PEACEFUL WAYS, LIKE SPEAKING OUT. HE ORGANIZED PEACEFUL MARCHES. MORE AND MORE

PEOPLE CAME. THEY STOPPED GOING TO WORK. THEY STOPPED BUYING BRITISH PRODUCTS.

IN 1947, INDIA BECAME A FREE COUNTRY. PEOPLE CHEERED IN THE STREETS. THEY CHEERED FOR GANDHI, THEIR GREAT LEADER. THEY CALLED HIM THE FATHER OF THE NATION.

Her father watched proudly from the first row.
Beside him, her mother wiped tears from her eyes
as she listened to her daughter. Like her husband,
Tor Pekai had always believed in education for girls.

But Malala's struggle for the rights of women and girls had changed her, too. Tor Pekai was going to school now. She had learned to read and write. She was studying hard to speak English. Malala was helping her with her homework.

MOTHER TERESA (1910–1997)

MOTHER TERESA WAS A ROMAN CATHOLIC NUN WHO DEVOTED HER LIFE TO HELPING THE NEEDIEST PEOPLE IN INDIA. MOST WERE VERY POOR. SOME WERE TOO SICK TO WALK. SHE STARTED A SCHOOL IN THE CITY OF CALCUTTA (NOW KNOWN AS KOLKATA) AND TAUGHT ANY CHILD WHO WANTED TO LEARN. SHE OPENED A HOSPITAL AND TREATED PEOPLE WHO COULD NOT PAY. SHE FOUND FOOD FOR ANYONE WHO WAS HUNGRY, AND OFTEN WENT HUNGRY HERSELF SO THEY COULD EAT. PEOPLE CAME FROM ALL OVER INDIA. NO ONE WAS EVER TURNED AWAY. IN 1979, SHE WAS AWARDED THE NOBEL PEACE PRIZE.

That night, news
programs all over the
world showed film
clips of Malala's
speech. Like Gandhi,
Martin Luther King Jr.,
and Nelson Mandela
before her,
Malala had
started a
peaceful movement
to bring about change.
"Education is the
only solution," she
had said. "Education first."

NELSON MANDELA

Chapter 9
A Girl with a Book

Life had changed very fast for Malala. When she was eleven, she had spoken to local reporters about what was happening in the city of Mingora. On her sixteenth birthday, people everywhere had listened as she spoke at the United Nations. Three months later, her best-selling book, *I Am Malala*, was published. Copies were sold all over the world. A shorter version for children was published the next year.

On October 10, 2014, the Nobel Committee announced the winners of the Nobel Peace Prize.

This prize is awarded to people who do something to make the world a better place. In 2014, Malala Yousafzai, age seventeen, of Pakistan, was chosen

to share the Nobel Peace Prize. The other winner was Kailash Satyarthi (KAY-lash sah-tee-AR-tee), age sixty, of India. The committee was honoring them "for their struggle against the suppression of children and young people and for the right of all children to education."

KAILASH SATYARTHI

THE NOBEL PRIZE

ALFRED NOBEL WAS A SWEDISH CHEMIST AND INVENTOR. HE WAS BORN IN 1833 AND DIED IN 1896. HE WROTE PLAYS AND POETRY. HE ALSO INVENTED DYNAMITE AND BECAME VERY RICH. IN HIS WILL, HE STATED THAT MOST OF HIS MONEY WOULD GO TO PEOPLE WHO HAD HELPED TO CHANGE THE WORLD IN IMPORTANT WAYS. THE PEACE PRIZE WAS TO BE GIVEN TO WHOEVER HAD DONE THE MOST TO BRING ABOUT PEACE.

ALFRED NOBEL

THE NOBEL PRIZES ARE AWARDED EACH YEAR FOR THE GREATEST ACHIEVEMENTS IN PHYSICS, CHEMISTRY, MEDICINE, LITERATURE, ECONOMICS, AND PEACE. THE PRIZES ARE PRESENTED ON DECEMBER 10, THE ANNIVERSARY OF ALFRED NOBEL'S DEATH.

Malala was the youngest person ever to win a Nobel Prize. Her heroes Martin Luther King Jr., Mother Teresa, and Nelson Mandela had won the Nobel Peace Prize in years before her.

Malala was in chemistry class in Birmingham when she heard that she had won the prize. It was 10:15 a.m. A teacher came into her classroom and told her.

So what did Malala do?

She stayed at school. She went to her physics and English classes. She decided it should be a normal day. But of course, it wasn't a normal day!

Malala was happy to share the prize with Kailash Satyarthi. He was from India and had done much to stop children from being sold into slavery. There had been tension between India and Pakistan, Malala's homeland, in the past. Perhaps they could work together to try to create friendship between their countries. When she heard that they had won, Malala said, "One is from Pakistan. One is from India. One believes in Hinduism. One strongly believes in Islam. And it gives a message to people, gives a message to people of love between Pakistan and India and between different religions. And we both support each other. It does not matter what's the color of your skin, what language do you speak, what religion you believe in. It is that we should all consider each other as human beings."

On December 10, 2014, Malala and Kailash shared the stage at the Nobel Prize Award

Ceremony in Oslo, Norway. In her speech Malala said, "This award is not just for me. It is for those forgotten children who want education. It is for those frightened children who want peace. It is for those voiceless children who want change."

KAILASH SATYARTHI

KAILASH SATYARTHI WAS BORN IN THE CITY OF VIDISHA, IN THE CENTER OF INDIA. WHEN HE WAS A BOY, HE SAW MANY CHILDREN WHO COULD NOT GO TO SCHOOL. THEIR FAMILIES WERE VERY POOR, AND THE CHILDREN WERE FORCED TO WORK. SOME WORKED LONG HOURS IN FACTORIES. OTHERS WERE SENT AWAY TO WORK IN DISTANT COUNTRIES. LIKE MALALA, KAILASH LOVED SCHOOL AND COULDN'T IMAGINE NOT BEING ABLE TO LEARN. HE AND A FRIEND ASKED PEOPLE TO GIVE AWAY OLD BOOKS. IN ONE DAY, THEY COLLECTED ALMOST TWO THOUSAND. THEY PUT THEM IN A BOOK BANK FOR CHILDREN, RICH AND POOR, TO BORROW AND READ. WHEN HE GREW UP, KAILASH DEVOTED HIS LIFE TO RESCUING YOUNG CHILDREN WHO WERE BEING FORCED TO WORK. HE HAS SAVED MANY THOUSANDS OF CHILDREN. IN 1998, HE ORGANIZED A MARCH TO CALL ATTENTION TO CHILDREN AROUND THE WORLD WHO WERE BEING FORCED TO WORK INSTEAD OF GOING TO SCHOOL. MORE THAN SEVEN MILLION PEOPLE PARTICIPATED IN 103 COUNTRIES.

Like all Nobel Prize winners, Malala received a gold medal and prize money. Her part of the money—more than half a million dollars—would go into the Malala Fund, which helps children all over the world receive an education. The Malala Fund raises money to build and repair schools. It makes sure that there are safe places where young girls who were forced to work or marry can learn and study. It helps girls speak up for their right to go to school.

Now Malala's name and face with her shy, beautiful smile are known around the world. She never planned on being famous. There was only one thing that Malala really wanted. It was something that most children take for granted. It was something worth fighting for: the right to go to school.

TIMELINE OF
MALALA YOUSAFZAI'S LIFE

1997 —— Malala Yousafzai is born in Mingora, Pakistan, on July 12

2008 —— Speaks to local reporters about girls' schools closing in Mingora

2009 —— The blog *Diary of a Pakistani Schoolgirl* is published on the BBC Urdu website
Mingora girls' schools closed by the Taliban

2011 —— Awarded Pakistan's National Youth Peace Prize

2012 —— Shot by the Taliban on October 9
Family moves to Birmingham, England
The Malala Fund is started

2013 —— Awarded the Dutch KidsRights International Children's Peace Prize
Speaks to the United Nations Youth Assembly on July 12, her sixteenth birthday. It is Malala Day at the United Nations
Autobiography, *I Am Malala*, is published

2014 —— Awarded the Nobel Peace Prize with Kailash Satyarthi of India on December 10
Young readers edition of *I Am Malala* is published

TIMELINE OF
THE WORLD

Princess Diana is killed in a Paris car crash — **1997**

Google is founded — **1998**

After the 2000 election, the US Supreme Court decides — **2000**
that George W. Bush will become the forty-third
US president

Al-Qaeda terrorists hijack four planes and carry out — **2001**
attacks on the World Trade Center and the Pentagon on
September 11

The Iraq War begins — **2003**

President George W. Bush begins his second term — **2005**

Apple releases the iPhone — **2007**

Barack Obama is elected the first African American — **2008**
president of the United States

Osama bin Laden, the mastermind behind the — **2011**
September 11 attacks, is killed by US special forces
in Pakistan

US president Barack Obama is reelected — **2012**

Pope Benedict XVI announces his resignation — **2013**

Taliban gunmen invade a school in Peshawar, Pakistan, — **2014**
killing at least 141 people, mostly children

BIBLIOGRAPHY

"Class Dismissed: Malala's Story," accessed January 4, 2015, http://www.nytimes.com/video/world/asia/100000001835296/class-dismissed-malala-yousafzais-story.html.

* Gigliotti, Jim. **Who Was Mother Teresa?** New York: Grosset & Dunlap, 2015.

"Malala Yousafzai: 'Our books and our pens are the most powerful weapons,'" last modified July 12, 2013, accessed January 4, 2015, http://www.theguardian.com/commentisfree/2013/jul/12/malala-yousafzai-united-nations-education-speech-text.

"Malala Yousafzai's speech at the Youth Takeover of the United Nations," accessed January 4, 2015, https://secure.aworldatschool.org/page/content/the-text-of-malala-yousafzais-speech-at-the-united-nations/.

* Rau, Dana Meachen. **Who Was Gandhi?** New York: Grosset & Dunlap, 2014.

*Books for young readers

Yousafzai, Malala, and Christina Lamb. **I Am Malala: The Girl Who Stood Up for Education and Was Shot by the Taliban**. New York: Little, Brown and Company, 2013.

* Yousafzai, Malala, and Patricia McCormick. **I Am Malala: How One Girl Stood Up for Education and Changed the World**. New York: Little, Brown and Company, 2014.

WEBSITES

www.bbc.com

www.malala.org

www.nobelprize.org

www.npr.org

105